11 Beautiful Tools: The Social Media Success Guide for Beauty Professionals

Terez D. Baskin

DEDICATION

This book is dedicated to my family and friends. Thank you for all your love and support. Sharon, Ricardo, Paul, Stella, Naiya, Corey Sr., Corey Jr., Betty, and my dearly departed Thelma.

ACKNOWLEDGMENTS

My Sisters Janell, Lisa, Stella, Mika and Carmen.
Every nephew.

Then there is the Fantastic 4. Laila McCloud, Jade, Nakeisha
Leveston-Jones. My Aunts: Mildred, Sandra, Alana, & Gwen.
Candice and Krissy.

I want to thank my brother Ken for being
the amazing designer for this project and so many others.
Thank you for being best big brother a girl from Maywood could
ever have. There is no one I would rather fight for and fight with.
Your talent always humbles me.

The Makeup Show Chicago,
James Vincent, Crystal Wright, Michael Duenas,
Francesca Alexander, and Julie Mahloch for all your support of this
project. All the Beauty Bloggers, Makeup Artists, Manicurists, and
Hair and Fashion Stylists I have met along the way.
You keep the world a beautiful place.

CONTENTS

My Introduction to Your Greatness
Let's catch lightning in a bottle

"You are the thunder and I am the lightning. Naturally."

—*Selena Gomez*

Your work as a beauty professional is a labor of love. You love color. You love the story it creates. You love contour. You love innovation. You love the perfect curl. You love a phenomenal eyebrow arch. You relish in details, like what type of bristles are in a blush brush. You know a kabuki brush from a blending brush. You love the lights of a vanity.

You are keenly aware of your perfect shade, be it warm tones, cool tones, the fairest beige to the darkest chocolate. You love skin, hair, nails, and by direct extension you love the artistry involved with each. These are the canvases you use to create magic. If these descriptions make your heart race, then I got your number. I am a fashion girl myself, but I have a special place in my heart for beauty artistry—your God-given ability to "beat" a face and transform the human body into its best self. Your talent has led you from the love of curls to a beauty entrepreneur.

A brand.

My hat is forever tipped to your talent. Yet, no matter how talented you are, or how fantastic you make me look, your talent—your artistry—is perishable.

As an artist, you may have "beat" a breathtaking face yesterday, but today no one would know it. You are Clark Kent without the cape. Unknown to the rest of us outside of your cape (smock), your heroic qualities are hidden. This work, your extraordinary life's work, is the lightning. Your greatness is hard to capture. But it is only hard to catch if you are not diligent in driving your career forward with social media. Without it, the lightning is lost. And in the great words of Selena Gomez it should come naturally.

That's what *11 Beautiful Tools* is for. It's here to help you catch lightning in a bottle.

Lightning in a bottle.

Capturing something powerful and elusive and then being able to hold it and show it to the world. You are performing a rare feat by sharing a moment of creative brilliance.

In this book, you will be given practical information and easily applicable action items that can be used as you read, tasks that you can accomplish right now. For example, tweet this quote:

"Share and they will come...#11BeautifulTools via @TerezBaskin"

Take a photo for Instagram. What does your day look like? Share the glamour life!

Upload it to Facebook. Go ahead, I can wait!

Welcome back! In the old days being a beauty pro meant doing work and waiting for some sign the work existed. After a photo shoot, you would wait for proofs or prints to be developed. You would wait months for the magazine to be published. Your tear sheets were in the mail. Now that you live in an Instagram world, shareable moments happen all the time. *Look at this bun. Did you see those bangs or ponytail? Her nails look fierce. Honey, you look snatched. Your eyebrows look flawless. Red lipstick is in! Have you seen this new Chanel nail polish in mint?!*

You see, every action of your industry life can be on display in real-time. This instantly connects you with your peers, and impresses those in a position to hire, which is crucial because you want to be employable. Your portfolio is everything, and now everything is your platform to display your fabulousness.

Each chapter will give you action items and strategies to get you started while you read. This book isn't just about theory. This book is to get you moving in the right direction. You will see examples of good status updates, video, vines, etc. At the end of each chapter, you will be given platform-specific tasks. These tasks will assist you in applying the information presented with each tool. I want you to feel accomplished before you move on the next platform.

Permission:

You are the expert. Do you realize the difference between you and a famous beauty blogger is mindset? They are fearlessly using the digital space to make you look bad. Not on purpose. You are the one with the training. You are the one with the know-how. You are the one doing the work daily. I understand that this journey maybe new and different, but it is our current business landscape.

I am fully aware that even this book has a shelf life. It will not be relevant in twenty years, but it is essential today. This is the time to take advantage of what other industries are already doing. I give you permission to be the expert online that you already are offline.

Be willing and ready to make mistakes. As a blogger, I make plenty of mistakes. There are platforms you can try and test and use. There will be some here you won't use at all. I understand that. I am writing to you from my heart and the humanity of imperfection. These are tips, tricks, and tactics I've learned along the way.

My eight years experience in social media—of trial and lots of errors—has taught me that it is okay to work it out while you are working. This text is not intended to solve all of your problems, but it will help you leapfrog and accelerate your success. I would be a liar if I said that after reading this, you are guaranteed to earn a ten-thousand-dollar a month advertising deal, or you will get you work in a major magazine in three months. Have these things happened for my clients? YES. It happened because they were willing and ready to do the work. By reading this, I hope you have decided that you want to be taken seriously as a beauty professional. Using the digital landscape to your advantage will get you where you want to go.

Please sign below:

I agree to work my ass off on building my business online.

X_____

You, Beauty Professional

X_____

I, Terez Baskin am always here to help.

Now that we agree to get serious, turn the page toward your future.

Tool - 1

the FACEbook

When I started using the Facebook in 2005, this is exactly what it was called then, "The Facebook." It was a barbaric site with pictures of people I did not know. I got an invite by a coworker who was an East Coast transplant to Chicago. Being away from her friends, Facebook was the quickest way to see what they had done the night before at that party they attended. She was my first friend. And unlike Tom from MySpace, I knew nothing about this platform and no one using it. I posted a photo from a recent photo shoot, as my profile picture and left. In 2005, I was knee-deep in planning and preparation for the Miss Black Illinois pageant. All my efforts and attention were on choosing the right song to sing in the talent competition. I needed to gather all the right clothes and look the part of a pageant princess. I thought Facebook might be a good way to encourage donations, but to my surprise no one I knew was using it. I reverted back to the safe zone of MySpace.

I stayed away for months. I never changed that smiling young Facebook photo of a pre-pageant queen. Yet as my reign as Miss Black Illinois 2005, I needed to raise money for my national pageant. As the national pageant neared, in Washington DC, I decided to dust off my password and connect with my entire pageant sister group. You know, to get a look at the competition! After the pageant, we stayed connected. We shared a snapshot in history, which no one else understood. We were no longer competitors, now we were comrades. Long rehearsals in heels while hungry. Smiling when you did not want to. Shaking hands when you had to, and pretending to love it. Even my favorite story of the entire experience was farcical at best. Twenty-five of the best damn twenty-something women filing hand in hand into a popular DC night club, like it was our second-grade trip to the city zoo. We were quarantined to VIP by security and only able to dance with each other. Over the years as Facebook grew. My friend requests did also.

Facebook is no longer barbaric. And if it were a country it would be the eleventh biggest in the world.

Here is why it matters to you.

People from all over the world are using it. Your customers are already on Facebook, and you probably are too. I am about to shift your mindset into the Facebook for business world. Facebook is one vast social story. A story of all the things you love (likes), and folks who have the potential to buy (friends). Your product is your skills and talents as a beauty professional, and you should be taken seriously. If you are just using Facebook to connect with people from high school you didn't even like back then, you are wasting valuable time and money on a tool that is not working for you. Yes, you are wasting money. Everyone not making money using social media is wasting money.

Once you've passed the point of just playing with people's hair to have your own salon or hair products line; to playing dress-up on dolls to styling the stars like Rachel Zoe. I know what you are thinking there is a lot of in-between steps. I know, but I want you to understand that Facebook is the way to launch that dream. It is a digital way to start connecting the dots of the empire now. It is the digital outpost for all of your content.

Why you need to have a Page?

Pages are your Facebook-owned digital business. Don't get it twisted, if Facebook goes away tonight you will have nothing. Mark Z will have all your photos, friends, and all your likes, and you will have a sad panda face. Facebook is again just an outpost. A necessary filling station where you can sell goods and services, but essentially you want to drive people back to your home base. Your website or blog, but we will go deeper into that later. They used to be known as Fan Pages, but are now just plain ole Pages. It is the place that people come specifically to learn about what you do as a beauty professional. You may be tempted to share all of your hard work on your personal Facebook account, however, only your mama may like it. Pages are the place that you can be free to talk about your products, services, and money. This is where you want to capture your market (audience). Updates about your latest events can be housed here and connect people who need to know. This is your sales floor. You want to keep fresh content there. Tell people what you offer offline. You want to give updates to your fans/friends that are friendly, fun, and professional. No one here wants to see your ratchet photos of you falling down drunk last night. A. Not cute and B. It will hurt your brand. Once you've build a sizeable page you can start to grow all of your social networks.

On your page, you can:
- *Ask questions*
- *Post the latest video about that exciting new seasonal color story*
- *Industry news*
- *Photos, lots of PHOTOS*
- *Share updates about your business*

This is by no means an exhaustive list, but it is a good foundation.

Terez Tip #1: Here is my soapbox about photos. They must be clear, focused, and the best damn photos you've ever taken. Every time. If you are not good at taking photos, get good at taken them. This is FACEBOOK, and we are looking at every detail and scrolling through your friend's timeline. Better photos always draw in people.

Tasks & Takeaways: Facebook.

1. **Search Facebook for your ideal name.** As the platform has grown, your ideal name may already be taken. Be sure to create a page that is unique to your brand

2. **Create a profile.** The logistics of getting a great page is all about the images. Here is a straightforward image-sizing guide for most of the platforms this book with cover. Bookmark it. How to size images on social media: A cheat sheet | Articles | Home http://ow.ly/kaEqa

3. **Choose a category.**

4. **Make your name simple and easy to find.** For example, my

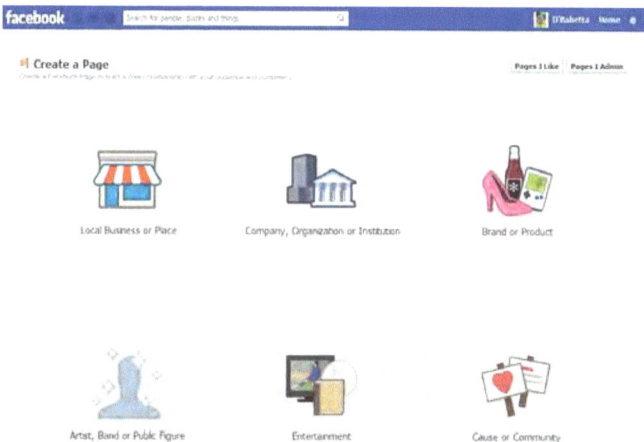

blog is called D'Babetta. My fan page is called D'babetta. My URL is Dbabetta.com. I have a Twitter handle specifically for the page @Dbabetta. I am always partial to using your name. It builds name recognition and brand awareness. Don't try to be too clever and miss the mark on being professional. Numbers and symbols are best left to your bank password. You don't want to be hard to find. It is better to be clear and consistent over multiple platforms to help your brand/name spread.

5. **Add fresh content daily.** As you are getting started, be sure

Terez Tip #2: This tip also works well with profile images/ avatars. Using the same photos on various platforms creates brand awareness. Changing you profile photo too often confuses your audience. You want to become recognizable in your community's timeline.

to share entertaining information that people want to read, like, and share. This will help grow your community and set the tone on what people can expect to get from your page.

6. **Plan out posts in advance.** Planning ahead will help you when you get busy behind the chair, and going about the business of your artistry in real life. Schedule one day a week to set up your posts for the upcoming week. You will also want to fill in with fresh content live, but you don't have to be on Facebook for fifteen hours a day to make a significant impact on your business.

7. **Allow an open community.** People may ask you questions. Be willing to talk to them. Don't just post and dash. Make sure you use Facebook efficiently. Check a couple of time a day to connect with people who may have liked or left com-

ments. Don't think everyone will pay for your expertise. Be willing to give free advice. It sometimes takes a long time for people to jump from interest to customer. It is okay, continue to nurture the community and it will pay off in the end.

Terez Tip #3: Choose your name wisely because once you get a hundred likes it is difficult to change the name.

Here is a resource that could help you get through those challenging negative comments online.
Negative Comment: How to Handle Negative Comments by author Gabby Bernstein http://ow.ly/kNPwZ

Tool - 2

How Tweet It Is!

Terez
@TerezBaskin

When you aren't clear. It makes it hard for people to know how to work with you. BUY From you. #Branding #BLMGirlExperience

↩ Reply   🗑 Delete   ⭐ Favorite   ⮂ Buffer   ↩ Storify   ••• More

4
RETWEETS

8:53 PM - 20 May 13

Twitter is like drinking from a river. You will never be able to retain it all, but it is possible to get what you need. Twitter was first called a micro-blogging site, but it is getting to your audience in less than 140 characters. This limitation can be good and it can be bad. Because it is limiting, it challenges you use the creative brain you already have. You want to strive for content that is fresh and easy for others to share. Twitter is built on the concept of share and share again. This is called retweeting. Retweeting is when you click the 🔁 button. Including someone in the conversation or tagging them in your tweet is called an at reply (@ reply). An @ reply is the quickest way to connect and be connected to anyone on Twitter. Following your interests is a good way to star to connect with people that are important to you.

When I got started on Twitter five years ago, it was a bunch of nerds (me included). We used it to gripe about work, and talk about what we ate for lunch. You may laugh, but in 2008, that is what we did. It was the digital wild wild west. As an early adopter, you could say almost anything, because so few people were going to see your content. I did. Now this platform is more sophisticated. It is in a word, useful.

As I write this about this tool, I hit my five-year Twitter anniversary. April 18, 2008. In five years I've grown with the platform. Have you ever heard of a fail whale? My uses have changed. My audience has changed. How I manage it has of course changed. Do not expect to get a million followers in a month, unless you are Beyonce's stylist and you start tweeting pictures of her looking Sasha Fierce. Your goal with any platform must be to connect, and be connected.

What I love about social media is the ability to take out limitations of geography and time. I follow and have connected with many international bloggers and brands because I use the platform to get work done. You can too, I will teach you how. Using Twitter for me is an essential component of my business objective. I know the power of the platform. I know you may think it is a silly thing, but it can absolutely lead to new opportunities.

Terez
@TerezBaskin

When you have a dream...Wake up and get to work.

← Reply ⟲ Retweet ★ Favorite ≋ Buffer ← Storify ••• More

9 16 PM - 14 Mar 13

How to make an impact on your market?

If you are not already using Twitter, the best way to make a quick impact is to follow and engage with others in your industry. Go to search.twitter.com and type in "beauty". You will get a list of top brands, bloggers, and artists like yourself. Then down the rabbit hole, to start following people you like. Follow people you admire. Follow brands you want to work with. Following peers you know off-line are a great start, but I am going to challenge you to expand your reach beyond that.

I want you to follow and engage with your industry influencers and brands. One of the best part about Twitter is the direct access to the superstars in your industry. A makeup artist whose work you admire. The beauty brand you use and want to work with in the future. That person at the brand you have been trying to connect to via e-mail or in person. That influencer or industry insider is only 140 characters away. No gatekeepers here. Think of it as getting to call the direct line of the CEO at Brand X. Your goal should be to take advantage of that opportunity and be engaging in a memorable way.

No time to tweet: How to maximize Twitter in 20 minutes a day!

Repeat these steps twice a day, and you will be on your way to dominating your twitter timeline. You don't have to spend your entire day sucked into twitter to be a rock star at it.

1. 5 minutes scheduling updates for the day (I would encourage the once a week method).

   - 3–5 messages about upcoming events.
   - Tips.
   - Article links.
   - Ask questions.

2. 3 minutes responding to @replies.

   - Give great follow-up responses to people who have connected with you since you last logged on.
   - Be fun and entertaining.
   - Thank people who connect with you in a way that is personal (take the time to see who and what they are about).
   - If new followers are relevant to your community follow them back.

3. 2 minutes watching your timeline.

   - Retweet things you find interesting or relevant to your community and followers.
   - Comment on images or others' work, you think would be awe-inspiring or fun.
   - Use this time to grow your network by following through on conversations of people you follow, find out who they talk to.
   - Get in on the action! Don't be afraid to jump into a conversation and @reply someone who shared something you liked or enjoyed.

Audience analysis.

I need you to think critically about how you segment your community. There are supporters, engaged members, and influencers. Every eco system is made up of this core cast of characters. When you are at a photo shoot, you have an integral part to getting the work done even though you are the one taking the picture. Right? Well let's go over the three distinct audiences every brand online has in common. You have friends, colleagues, and customers. You have to learn to be the court jester to all three. What you want to do is get to a place where you have permission with these audiences to be uniquely you every day. Meaning you can go off topic or off brand and not have your follower number drop like the stock market because you mentioned something you are passionate about. Training your audience is key to brand recognition. Start with a clear and consistent objective for each audience. This can also be duplicated across multiple platforms in your beauty professional tool belt. The goal should not just be to grow your numbers. Clear objectives are about the end goals you have for your career and business. These goals should be greater than the platform and be about your business. I will raise awareness about my skills (specialty). Be an expert at something. I am sure there is something you relish in doing and are really great at it. That is what you focus on. Do not waste your time with topics you are just okay at.

Friends – People who you know in real life (IRL) or online. These updates may be more personal. They may have a more relaxed tone. They may be funnier and more playful with a relaxed yet professional tone. Your customers are still watching. Don't act like they aren't looking because you said the word shit online. But realize these platforms are used for business and you would never throw trash in someone's face. Don't do it online either.

Colleagues – This group is made up of other professionals at your level or other levels. Whether you are a recent cosmetology grad or a seasoned industry professional, treat others in your industry like peers and with respect. They are either individuals you can learn from or individuals you can teach. You need to see other professionals as the network that will help you leapfrog forward. They may be the best teachers and have great examples. You can learn by their mistakes. Ask yourself: Are they somewhere you want to go?

> ***Terez Tip #4***: Think of how you can move a relationship off this quick platform. Do you have a blog you can ask them to read? Do you have a web portfolio that you can direct them to? Can they get more community engagement from the great Facebook Page you just created? Yes. Yes. Yes. This is how you fill your offline business funnel.

Help others find resources. Refer people by @replies. Comment on the work of others. People like the go-to person who's willing to give them solid expert information. Don't let bloggers have all the fun. You are a trained professional, be fearless and go for it.

Customers – People who will and can purchase your products, and services. They want to connect with you to understand more about your expertise. Your experience and passion for artistry is what will draw them in. We want the view from behind the chair. You may have shown me a smoky eye or a blending technique, and I may not master it, but what if I could just pay you to do it.

Investing your time wisely can yield exponential benefits to your brand and your offline beauty business. You won't be making the hard sell on the outpost. You will be leading them to your online home where the sale happens.

However you are selling via social media. You are selling yourself, you the artist. You are selling your brand. People will decide to buy based on the quality of your work and the digital image you project. They will make a snap decision about whether they will buy from you based on your online presence.

Help me out: #hashtags.

Hashtags are used on several social media platforms. They were revolutionized on Twitter as a way to organize conversations, track topics, and brand mentions. Hashtags are now a part of our social media understanding, but many don't know how to use them effectively. They can be used on Google+, YouTube, Twitter, Instagram, Vine, and Pinterest. At the time of publishing Facebook has just released a beta test of hashtags on the site. Not ever user has them.

Hashtags help categorize your conversations on twitter. They are also cross channel marketing and can be used on Google+, Instagram, Pinterest, and just recently Facebook. You are still unable to search one hashtag and yield results from all platforms at this time. Below is a great link to a resource article that will help you understand hashtags and how they can move your information along. There are great websites like Hashtags.org that could help you in understand the depth of proper hashtags and their importance to you as a beauty brand. I happen to love how hashtags add me to a larger conversation that is searchable.

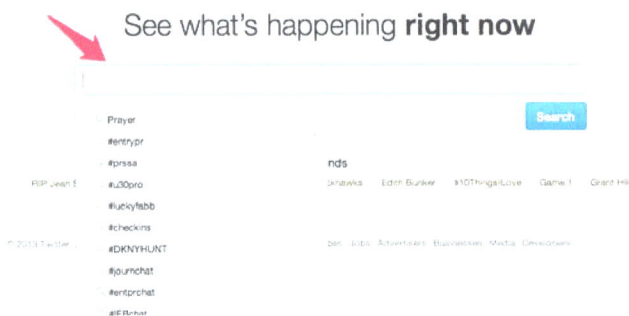

Go back to search.twitter.com and search these topics and track your results

#beauty_____   #hair_____

#makeupartist_____   #nails_____

Are you surprised by what you found?

Shop talk.

Twitter chats are the digital version of shop talk. I make lots of connections with friends, colleagues, and customers during that time. Twitter chats are live twitter events by a specific host or group of people who will share content, ask questions, and provide information around the same hashtag. Recently, I found #Beautychat. I don't know who the creator of this chat is, but it seems to be every Friday afternoon at 2:00 p.m. EST.

On chats you will find bloggers, beauty lovers, and beauty professionals like you, ready to gab about the latest and greatest beauty information and trends.

You can answer people's burning beauty questions or point them to online resources.

Every interaction should show you being the expert. Treat this as your time to show off your skills.

Terez Tip #5: Find a chat and jump on it. You will gain followers. You will expand your Twitter reach and position yourself as an industry expert. Include chats to the list of all of the online activities that you do to help your offline business grow. It is free advertising for what you do in real life as a beauty pro.

How to Tweet with Intention

56 Terez @TerezBaskin   25 May
Your Beauty Secrets Revealed in the #BeautyBooth :
buff.ly/10Vmgfr via @Dbabetta cc: @GlossedandFound
@Ulta_Beauty
Expand

56 Terez @TerezBaskin   25 May
@glossedandfound @Dbabetta @ULTA_Beauty thanks for the RT
Hide conversation
← Reply   🗑 Delete   ★ Favorite   ← Storify   ⇄ Buffer   ••• More

4:50 PM - 25 May 13 📍 from Maywood, IL · Details

Reply to @glossedandfound @Dbabetta @ULTA_Beauty

Name 5 brands you use in your work:

1. _____

2. _____

3. _____

4. _____

5. _____

Take a photo on your next shoot or on your next job of that brand's product in your tool kit, or your makeup bag. Write down their Twitter handles here:

1. _____

2. _____

3. _____

4. _____

5. _____

Make sure you mention these Twitter handles in your next tweet and also mention them on Instagram. Find three brands and follow them. If you use their products, @mention them with your photo in the update.

1. _____

2. _____

3. _____

Terez Tip #6: Be sure to search on Instagram for the business handle. Some brands are not yet using this tool, or the handle may be different from their Twitter account.

Tool - 3
Your YOUtube Classroom

Did you know that YouTube is the second largest search engine next to Google? Meaning people are using it to gain information and learn what you have to say. Let's be honest, you would watch a five-minute video rather than read a 1,500-word essay on the same topic.

I would too, and if we would, then chances are other people would watch a video as well. Video content is a fantastic way to showcase your artistry and talented teaching techniques in a three-dimensional way.

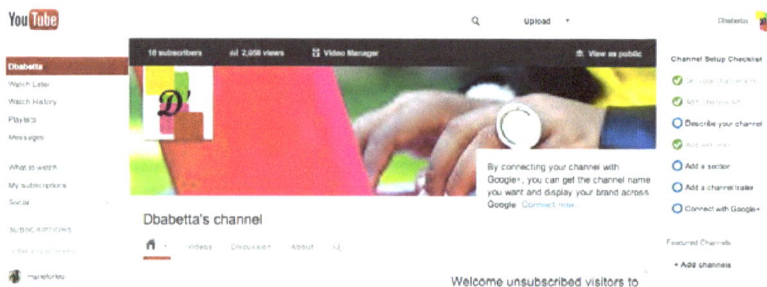

Here is why this matters to you: You are missing valuable money sitting on the sidelines. YouTube is like owning our own content-creation station. You are the producer, the writer, and more importantly the star. You are the expert. You know why applying eye makeup first is better than slathering on concealer and foundation.

> *Terez Tip #7*: Get over how you feel about your voice. Get over how you feel about your face. You need to get past all those crazy ideas about why you can't do video and get going.

Start in your salon or your living room and prop up a camera, and go. Then forget that the camera is there. Pretend that it is not there. Imagine that you are explaining this information to your grandmother. You want her to be able to hear your kind approach to the topic. You also want to be sweet and pleasant in your delivery. You will also need to speak up and project your words clearly, because grandma cannot hear so good anymore baby! Wink.

Your goal here is to put your artistry on display. The audience needs to hear your words clearly and see your example sharply.

Video content you control. You are the star!

- *Teach people your skills*
- *Highlight your techniques*
- *Give tips and tricks*
- *Talk about trends*
- *Celebrity looks*
- *Recreate a look from a magazine*
- *Share the tools to help create a look*

Channel content consistency

A lot of content marketers I read and public relations industry people like to say phrases like, "Content is King". The truth is, consistency is king. When you start to use these tools and gain a following they start to count on that information you provide. The best way to build a loyal audience and create a community that will support your career is to be consistent. This is so true for video content. People will feel an affinity toward you because they hear your voice. They are in on the inside joke of who you are. Let your personality radiate through their screen. Don't leave them hanging for a long time. You know the feeling when you favorite show is on hiatus. This is how your fans will feel about your absence on screen.
Lauren Elizabeth a big Youtube darling said I tries to post one video a week, "otherwise people think I am dead." You don't have to be that serious, but keeping an up to date video channel is important.

I realize that this can be difficult when you have a lot of offline business and good stuff happening in your real life. Share this with your subscribers, they want to share in your wins. Try short update videos about what you are up to if you don't have time for a full-length video.

The beauty sweet spot.

The video tutorials you are going to create can be extremely detailed in real-time or edited down by steps. It is your choice to decide what you are comfortable with based on your skill level. If you are just starting out on YouTube they will limit the length of the videos you can upload. Overtime as your channel grows, YouTube will extend this limit in increments. You will eventually do live streaming of your "shows" through Google+ Hangouts! I will explain the value of this later, but know this is a great goal when you start a channel.

I love On Air Hangouts on G+; they allow you to engage in real-time with viewers.

I believe the shorter the video the better. Make sure you know what you want to teach or talk about in the video. Leave the ums or "I don't know why I am vlogging?" videos on the editing floor. The best way to build an audience is to have a solid video with great details and information that people can use right away.

Out of all of the tools in this book this is going to be the one that requires your full commitment. Yet, it can pay off for you the best. Your owned media is part of your total package portfolio and it could lead to bigger things like television opportunities. Each time you create a video think that you are on a national television show and who could potentially be watching.

Let's talk about search, baby.

As I mentioned, YouTube is one big searchable video catalog. It is run by the ultimate search machine, Google. In order to get good subscribers you have to help them find you. Depending on your special artistry, brainstorm some keywords you could use for your video tags and in your video titles. This is called Search Engine Optimization (SEO). By using terms that are often searched on the web that relate to your topic, people can find your expert information listed online. Use terms that are commonly searched to get better results for your awesome new video. The trick is to get good search results in a term that people are actually looking for.

> *Terez Tip #8*: In the description of each video drive people to other platforms! Did you use this video in a blog post? Link back to the content.

Be very detailed. Be sure to tag the brands you are using in the video in your description box. A list of these items with names would also be great for you. Add great SEO tags to get good search results for your videos. Be the first to share your own videos. Give them legs, by sharing them across your Twitter, Facebook. Load the videos to beauty niche sites like Beautylish and Bloom to get even more spread.

Channel surfing (YOUTube worksheet)

Research your audience and community: Find 5 channels your audience would watch.

1. _____

2. _____

3. _____

4. _____

5. _____

This is the time you can mirror what you like. But have a critical eye for what you dislike. . Avoid the things you think are not appealing to your brand. Be critical, but not gossipy. If the information is great, but the quality is poor then think of how you could improve those elements in your videos.

1. Name your channel using name or your business name.

   _____

2. Choose your category: How-to and Style (this will fit perfectly for beauty professionals).

3. Choose your video keywords

4. Add a channel description using SEO keywords

_____   _____

_____   _____

5. Make sure you add a channel trailer. This is a one-minute video about what to expect from this channel.

_____   _____

_____   _____

6. Upload a profile photo or channel logo. Remember to use a photo similar to your other social platforms.

7. Upload your first video.

8. Choose your best videos for your featured videos.

9. Don't post and dash. Check channel activity and reply to comments.

BLOOM

Tool - 4
Let Your Beauty Bloom.com

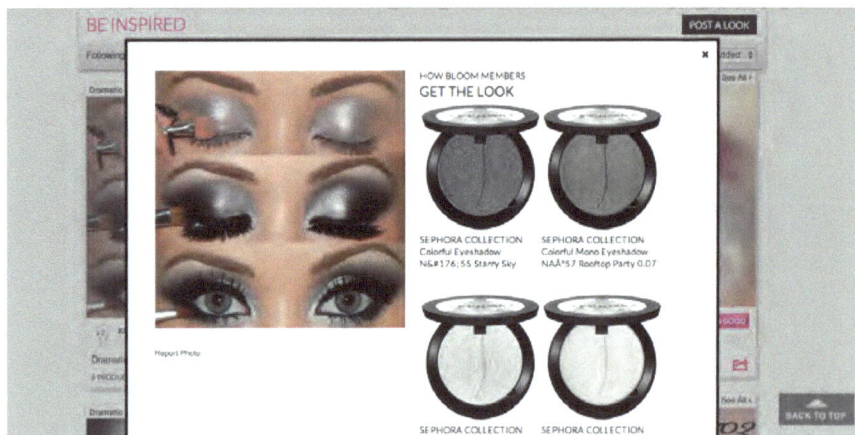

What if you had a platform that allowed you to have a real-time image resume? What if you could get business referrals from people who want to hire you for your talent? What if that platform allowed you to connect with brands by tagging their products from the images you upload? Sounds sweet right? It already exists in Bloom.com. I love Bloom. I believe the platform meets the needs of three key audiences: beauty brands, beauty professionals, and beauty lovers like you and me.

Brands can use the platform to grow brand awareness in a place where people who use their products inspire others to use the products. That means you are the expert. As the professional you are considered my beauty doctor. You are the expert on my hair, my eyebrows, my nails, and my skin. If you give me a recommendation it will hold the same weight as if my doctor told me take this vitamin, or my dentist saying don't eat this it will rot your teeth. Brands understand this influence is a key part of their business. Your recommendations directly drive sales. Putting products in your hands means products will make their way to consumers who need them and want them the most. Bloom is making this connection stronger with their platform where you can create content and link it back to the original seller, the brand. It is a win–win marriage between beauty brands and professionals. I, as the layperson, may not know why I need the item when I pass it on the store shelf at my beauty retailer. But if I see it in action on your visual content, then that is a different story. It may push me toward a purchase.

As a beauty lover, I use Bloom to stay current on trends. I may be driven to the site from different places, but I know I can always get the information about the brand unlike fawning over a great nail photo on Pinterest. I may never know what the name of that color is or the technique to achieve it. Prime example: I was at America's Beauty Show in Chicago this past winter.
I walk up to the massive China Glaze booth. I was so excited to see all the bottles lined up like little soldiers in a rainbow-colored army. I had no idea which color I was looking for. Bloom would have solved this problem. Weeks earlier I'd seen the cutest coral manicure on Pinterest, the blogger was clever enough to hold up a China Glaze bottle in the photo, but no name. On Bloom.com this photo could have been tagged with the China Glaze in the photo with the exact color name. What makes the brand happy is that consumers can click through to purchase it right from their e-commerce site.

Beauty professionals like you can build your content like a resume of looks. Create a lookbook from a specific event or trend. If you sign up for their pro account for a small fee, you can be listed as a professional in your area, which means I can search for you by location, and I can see right on your profile if you can create my desired look. For instance, I am out of town for a wedding. I need a color or cut, or nail services. I go to Bloom and search by city. I see what you are working with and I can contact you to book that service. Sweeter still is this platform keeps you connected to brand, buyers, and other industry professionals. This is your chance to show me what you are working with. You can also use this tool on the go with their mobile application for both iPhone and Android.

Beauty lovers like me can learn a new trend or technique. I can see a video of how-tos, I can take what I've learned and apply it by purchasing the products to get the look.

Let's fill your garden on Bloom.com

1. Create a profile on Bloom.com (Use your name or business name).

2. Upload a great cover image (this should be a logo or action shot).

3. Upload your social media profile image.

4. Update your profile information with your training and professional experience.

5. Start a lookbook.

6. Upload a video from your YouTube channel.

7. Become a vibrant community member by clicking the +*Looks Good* Button to show your support for other professionals.

> *Terez Tip #9*: A good profile picture highlights you as the centerpiece. Don't get artistic. Just a great shot of your face will help your potential clients and brand reps know who you are as an artist.

B

Tool - 5
Oh, Boy Beautylish-cious

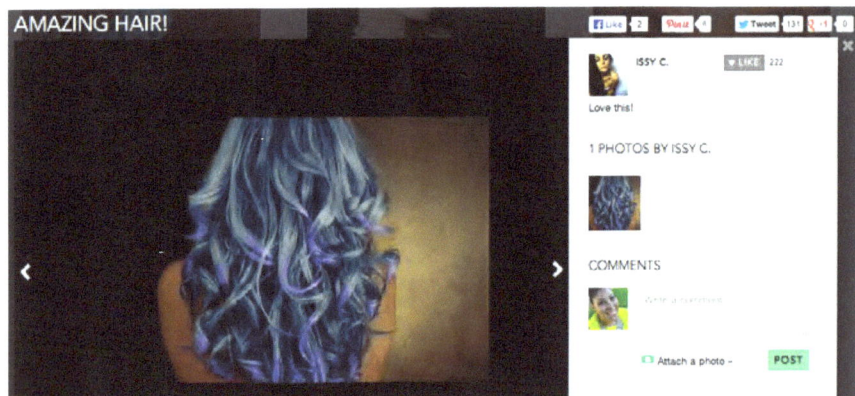

AMAZING HAIR!

ISSY C.　♥ LIKE 222

Love this!

1 PHOTOS BY ISSY C.

COMMENTS

Attach a photo –　POST

$\mathbf{B}$e editorial. Be ready to share your expertise with the world. Be ready to work what you know, this isn't a test. While Bloom is about showcasing your professional talents with consumers and lovers of beauty, Beautylish is about preparing you to be the best artist you can be, while some of those tips may spill over to me as a consumer and beauty lover. The true genius behind Beautylish is their ability to use master artists to get you ready for the industry and make you the best artist around. I first heard about Beautylish at the Makeup Show Chicago. I looked it over. I loved it. The best part about this platform is the tutorials. I learned how to put on false lashes. I share articles these articles constantly, when people in my community asked me how to do this or that. I go right to Beautylish and type in their question and send them the link. Over the last few years they have built an amazing catalog of content regarding beauty and lifestyle information. How do I do X? There is more than likely a great post or tutorial out there. How to do dramatic eye looks? Yep! How to get a cat-eye with liquid liner? Yep, that also!

What you will care about the most is the professional tips on this site that are just about making you a better artist. James Vincent, the director of artistry for The Powder Group has written a comprehensive series on "Building a Professional Makeup Kit." He continues to share his professional tips and tricks of the trade. He has made a name for himself in the industry as an artist, but he believes in giving back to newcomers through education.

The professional education aspect is the cornerstone of their business model. I can also tell you that there are tons of other well-known professionals and up-and-coming professionals who are building a name for themselves using this community to drive their popularity and artistry influence. Their tips are amazing. I could sit for hours learning more and more about how they make the magic happen.

Your opinion matters.

What they also do well is create a community like Amazon built on customer reviews. Talk about the products you use personally or professionally and tell me what you like, and more importantly do not like. Again, as a consumer your expert opinion matters. The other twist of Beautylish is that you can buy some really great products from the built-in store. This is where beauty do-it-yourselfers and professionals collide to make a great community, and create a volume of understandable and accessible information. Beautylish is where you as an artist expert can shine. On Bloom you can inspire. On Beautylish you can educate. Write great content on your blog and share the photos here to drive traffic back to your home base.

Here again are the three ways you can engage with the community on Beautylish:

1. Upload video and photo content (don't forget to tag the brands), which can drive traffic, back to your owned media spaces.
2. Review products you already use.
3. Share what other industry experts are teaching.

Become Beautylish-cious (Worksheet)

1. If you are not a member already, sign up for Beautylish.

2. Create a custom URL (for example: beautylish.com/Dbabetta).

3. Upload a profile picture (this should match your other social profiles).

4. Link to your other social networks: Facebook and website.

5. Enter your current contact information.

6. FAQs – This is an underrated piece of information, but what do your clients ask you often. This is your specialty, so answer a quick and easy question in the box.

7. Create a cool and unique headline.

8. Become a part of the community

   -Leave comments on Posts

   -Share information you read and love

   -Tag brands you like

   -Don't forget to shop

Terez Tip #10: Bio boxes can get you business. This is your thirty-second written commercial about you and your business. Make it good! Find a creative way to talk about yourself. Let people know how great you are in a simple and easy to digest way.

Tool - 6

Give Me Insta-GLAM

Instagram is the on-the-go glam capture machine. Allow this application to drive your beauty world. It is the backstage all-access pass to your fabulous life.

I know that there are great moments happening every day in your life as a beauty professional. Curate them via Instagram. Be careful of the images you present. They can help or hurt you. I tell people all the time I am a fashion blogger not a style blogger. The distinct difference is that I don't post daily photos of my outfit of the day. You might get that once a month or a quarter. But even on the days I am rocking a haute outfit, I may not post the entire look to Instagram. Why? Because I don't want to set the standard of showing off every outfit when I don't plan on continuing that practice. So on the days I look like a slug, in my college sweatshirt and khakis, you won't judge. That isn't inspiring. Be strategic in the digital life you present to Instagram. A well edited life can be just the thing to bolster your popularity in the digital space.

Instagram is the application revolutionizing mobile imaging. The filter aspect of the application makes even crappy out of focus photos into art. This tool allows shareable posts called a Re-gram similar to a Retweet on Twitter. People will share their lives and loves. What we say is one thing, but what we capture and share is another thing altogether. People on the surface know me on the net as a fashion and beauty social marketer, but my Instagram will tell the truth about me. I am a mom who makes homemade dinners several nights a week. You will see funny photos of my kids, but I am no mommy blogger. I am a mom who blogs, and there is a distinct, yet subtle difference. You also have to know exactly who you are. What do you specialize in? What do people ask you about the most? That is your specialty and what you are known for. Do not be the Jack-and-Jane-of all-trades. It is better to be a specialist. They get paid more.

They are able to write their own ticket. Experts are always asked for first, last, and all the time. Be an expert in your Instagram stream. Show people vibrant hair colors. Share that breathtaking blending technique. I want to see an ombre nail art photo. Let your pictures share a thousand words.

Your digital image diary.

- *Show off a daily look (hair, nails, colors)*

- *Recreate a look in the media*

- *Show me your setup for a photo shoot or job*

- *Behind-the-scenes photos of prep work for a big job*

- *Share your personality.*

Know your biz (protect your brand).

The newest trend in professional contracts are social media clauses. These clauses may stipulate that you cannot take a photo of the client. You may not take a picture of logos, or discuss the company/ brand you are working for. In these cases, it may get harder and harder to be creative, but being creative is what you do best. I read the comments, read between the lines, and I found out a major stylist I know was working on something MAJOR. He could not share that without blowing the deal. He was able to talk about the potential client and shared images of similar looks. Slick, right? He did not put the client in an awkward place by asking to take a photo, and he did not scoop any secret information. Bottom line, if you are not sure just ask.

Terez Tip #11: Here is a 360-degree approach to fill all of your social media buckets. Use Instagram photos on your blog, Twitter, Facebook, and still shots from your YouTube videos. You can use the same content, but personalize your approach for each platform

You know you love it. I can be honest and tell you I love it. Instagram is the easiest way to gain followers and drive people back to your business blog/site. It does a great job of highlighting your talent and sharing it to the world. It also does a great job of helping you align with other pros using hashtags.

Resource: How to Use Instagram (and its Hashtags) to Promote Your Brand http://ow.ly/kfDv9

Let's Get Video

Video has come to Instagram. The revolutionary image sharing site has added a video component that goes right at the throat of Twitter's Vine app. It was released in June 2013, and is still so new many are not sure how to use it. It boosts a 15 second video instead of Vine's 7 seconds and provides users with video only filters to tranform why we all love instagram in the first place. I think what will make this next generation instagram successful is the fact that the audience is already on Instagram where as it may be harder to grow your presence on Vine.

To learn more:
Instagram Debuts Video Sharing - SocialTimes
http://ow.ly/mgp7y

Tool - 7

Go Viral with Vine

Embed Post

Simple   Postcard

Choose size: **600px**   480px   320px

This platform is still so new, you don't know what to do. Well here's why I think it will be big and why you should care. Bought by Twitter and brought to the world in January 2013, this platform brings you the world of video madness in six-second intervals. It challenges your creativity and ability to as the slogan says, "Make a Scene." At the time of writing this book, this application is only available for iO6 devices by Apple. It allows users to create GIF-like looped videos. That can be shared via Twitter (of course), Facebook, and by embedding them on your blog platforms.

I love this highly addictive, still growing platform, as it keeps your attention far beyond the six-second rule. It makes incredible sharable content.

Tips to use Vine.

Since the Vine application limits your time to only short spurts, you need to use keywords and hashtags to do the work for SEO and organization purposes. Choose wisely. Hashtags help organize your content: #Beauty #Makeup #Artistry #Tutorials. These little helpers will take you right to the audience you want to reach on Vine as well as Twitter. You can share the videos on Facebook as well.

Take your Vine to go.

The best part about the most recent update to the platform is that you can embed these videos for use on your blog! I love this. Unlike Instagram you aren't limited to just use this platform to utilize your content. Try a six-second tutorial. Tough, but I think you could do it. Write out the steps of the look you want to achieve and just shoot each piece after you complete it.

Seven tips for Vine.

1. Do play with content.

2. Do keep it clean (you are building a brand).

3. Do make it funny and entertaining.

4. Do use hashtags to give your vines some SEO legs.

5. Do embed the #beauty relevant videos on your blog.

6. Do embed those videos via Pinterest.

7. Do make great behind-the-scenes videos of your beautiful life as an artist and professional.

Get started on Vine.

1. Download the Application (Apple iOS only).

2. Create a name using your business name or your name.

3. Connect to Facebook/Twitter accounts for easy content sharing.

4. Find some friends (yours or not). Chances are you may be one of the first in the industry testing this tool which means you can kick ass and dominate on a shiny new platform.

5. Get Vining.

6. Share it baby!

7. Go like and comment on other videos in the community.

Terez 11d ago

What lipstick do you normally wear?
@merrellhollis #TMSChicago

THE MAKE-UP SHOW 2013

Tool - 8

Be a Pinterest Pusher

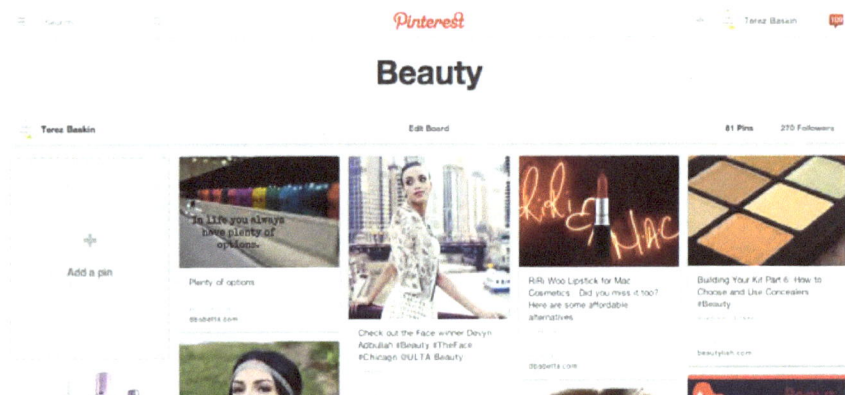

This is a lesson in digital sustainability. Pinterest is built on the solid principle of recycled, reused, and repurposed content, better known to you as viral content. Going viral means something's been shared million or so times. You may not need to go that high end to see the benefits of Pinterest on your beauty business. This is great when your image goes viral on Pinterest. Your brand-marketing plan has to include Pinterest as a large piece of the puzzle. All of the other tools are great for business, but this is a secret gold mine of the social scene. This large platform is 95% women. The beauty industry and therefore your customers are using this platform for inspiration and a destination to get information on what to purchase. It has overhauled the bridal industry, beauty, crafts, and fashion. Let's skip back to beauty. These buyers need to know you have something to sell. You are a service-based industry. Whether you do bridal make-up, hair, or nails, you pin down the money using Pinterest.

The BUYology.

According to Shopify.com, Pinterest customers spend on average eighty dollars. Think about your services. Do they cost more or less than eighty dollars? Even if they cost more, the point is that you can influence someone's buying decision based on what you post/pin to Pinterest.

Pinterest is a series of online bulletin boards that you can pin images (content) from across the web. So all those images you posted on Beautylish, videos you posted on YouTube, or all the lookbooks you uploaded to Bloom.com. Here is your chance to set a price tag to it. Think of each season, as its own seasonal section of your service offerings. I love talking about spring because it is just an easy time, and I hear birds chirping outside my window as I write this.

Your spring/summer Pinterest plan.
1. Set up or convert your account today at business.pinterest. com.
2. Verify your website. You may need a techy to do this for you, don't worry I did too.
3. Add the "Pin it" button to your blog/website.
4. Add a "Follow on Pinterest" Button to your blog/website.
5. Pin it to win it.

Terez Tip #12: Watermark your content with text, your logo, or website. As your pins travel the world you still want people to know that you are the original source. Use Picmonkey.com to add some text to your images or if you are fancy use Photoshop.

Pinterest strategy worksheet.

Come up with some catchy board names.

1. _____

2. _____

3. _____

4. _____

5. _____

Terez Tip #13: Name one of your boards TV. This can become a shareable library of all those great Youtube videos. For example: DbabettaTV

Brainstorm a seasonal list of items you could "sell" using Pinterest to drive traffic to your site.

1. _____

2. _____

3. _____

4. _____

5. _____

Brainstorm a list of good SEO tags for your description boxes.

1. _____

2. _____

3. _____

4. _____

5. _____

Tool - 9

G+

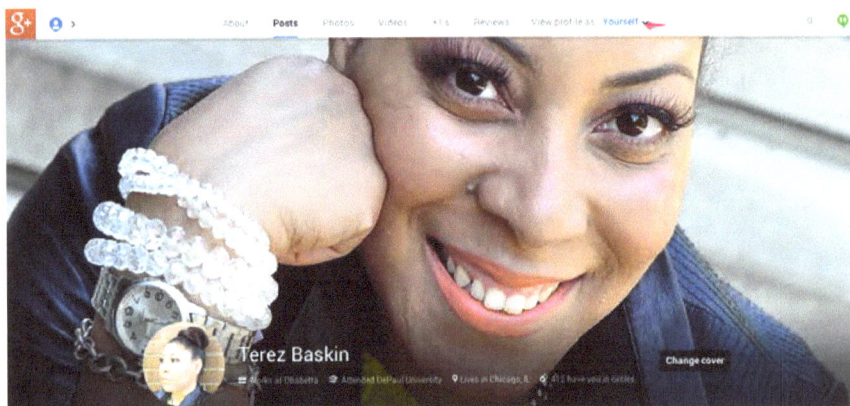

Just like YouTube, Google+ is the tool that has the most web power in your toolbox. This platform started by the search engine kings, gives you all kinds of Google juice, to the point that when you search your name in Google it will come up highlighted on the side of your search, if you have a Google+ profile. Google is the underdog of platforms because people are unsure how to use it, but leveraging this playground for content can change the way you are found online.

Circles

Google+ is a Google-based community that allows people to follow their likes or people and place them into circles. Google's community is built on circles. Meaning you can segment your content to the right circle for the job. Are you looking for a great blogger to partner with on a project? Great, you can send that just to your blogger circle. Want to share a more personal photo on the platform? You can just share it with your family and close friends circle. This helps you organize your content. It does have similar privacy settings and you can play around with what make the most sense to you.

What makes the most sense in business is an open network. I do understand the concept of circles for the G+ world, but what I will never understand is why you would have a business account on say Twitter or Instagram and make it a private account. If you believe that what you share is private then it deserves its own account. Making a business account private is like saying, "Don't buy from me. I don't want to interact with you anyway." For example, I have a circle for fashion, social media, and another one for photography.

Terez Tip #14: Google+ is one of the most powerful digital outposts. Because it is directly tied to Google. It will help your search rank in Google. We all want that coveted organic first page search love. Posting your updates here will help it spread more.

The circles help you to organize with whom and what you are talking about in each. Google+ can be connected to your YouTube channel to post videos; you can also do great live events using Google+ hangouts.

These have risen in popularity in 2012 and are still on track to be a growing force in live streaming media and content. Those in the tech world use them for weekly chats, much like a Twitter party/chat just in video format. This gives people a visual along with your words. You can still interact with the attendees via a chat box embedded within the hangout. Some use a hashtag and take the hangout across platforms and use Twitter to stay in on the hangout while exposing their fans and followers to the information they are learning or sharing. This is a great two-way channel idea to continue to grow your personal brand. I've presented in hangouts, organized hangouts, and attended hangouts.

I've created videos, not great ones, but decent enough to get you started on how to use Google+. More brands are using Google+ since the addition of Google+ Pages. They are the equivalent to Facebook Pages. Hangouts are for me, and should be for you, the best party on the web; your way to set yourself apart from what other people are doing, on a relatively new platform.

Google+ has been around for a few years, but I believe it has not even begun to catch the kind of fire I know it will when people thoroughly understand the value in how to use this powerful tool to connect. Hangouts are the best part of the community. They allow you to connect visually in real-time to a group of people. Google kicked it up even further by allowing your Google+ hangout to be broadcast live from your YouTube Channel. I think this is yet another way you can expand your digital brand to your customers.

Your beauty or lifestyle business needs to use this tool. It is one more item that can keep you relevant and connected. I have seen hangouts used for interviews. Is there another artist you want to feature on your site? This is the perfect way to connect with them and share it instantly with your audience. Live events have a vibe all their own. You can use that positive energy to boost your brand. If you are a makeup artist, you can use Google+ for online makeup demos. You can give tips on skincare and answer questions about your work. Are you a hairstylist? Well you can use Google+ hangouts to show off a new trendy technique. You can also answer questions about your hair care regime for clients or easy "how to get the look" videos. Your expertise is always needed and useful. Why not share your information while gaining new customers and clients in the process?

If you don't know, now you know.

Nearly 70 percent of people start the search for your business via Google, why wouldn't you want to further influence people's search efforts?

—Chris Brogan of ChrisBrogan.com

Pages

Google+ adds 625,000 users each day! This statistic is from 2012 and I am sure the number has increased since brand pages and verified accounts are growing. Verified accounts and vanity URLs came along in 2012 for celebrities and brands. I think a hangout is a great way to get the attention of that brand or magazine you want to work with. Social media takes away the barrier of the gatekeeper. You can go right to the editor online. Pages just like on Facebook can be managed by multiple people for posting and engagement. This is a great place to test as a new space to share content.

Trends, hashtags, and tagging.

Trends are similar to trending topics on Twitter. You can use hashtags to stay a part of a conversation. Tagging is easy if you want to use a brand or a product name in your update; you just put the + sign in front of it. This is like tagging in Facebook and drives people around the net and gives credit or information where it is due.

Getting started on Google+.

1. If you are already using Gmail as an e-mail provider then an additional sign-up is not required.

2. Upload a profile picture (the same for every other platform).

3. Upload a cover picture (much like you have on your Facebook page).

4. Add your professional contact information.

5. Add educational information.

6. Add a great headline.

7. Go and explore.

Hangouts

Google+ hangout is a video service that allows you to video chat in the Google+ community. I was on my very first hangout back in July of 2011, when people were curious about what this new way to connect that is Google+ was all about. Not to mention there were some pretty remarkable people on this hangout, an independent publisher of more than four hundred books; a novelist, who'd written three books in eighteen months (what an accomplishment), a photographer, and a music writer. Not as varied as a butcher, a baker, and a candlestick maker, but you get the gist.

This is what the web and social media can do. It connects people. It is the sole reason I love social media the way I do. I am connected and have connected with people I would otherwise never had the pleasure of knowing. I regularly contact bloggers in the UK; people who share my intense interest for fashion, beauty, and lifestyle information.

Y

Tool - 10
You.com
(Your digital real estate)

Y ou may own a home or rent an apartment in real life either is fine. I know you have storage for your tools; brushes, eye palettes, irons, clips, nail color galore, right? You spend so much time to take care of your offline life as you should. Now I want to talk to you about the importance of your online life. You need a home online. A place to call home. The place that no one can ever evict you from, or crash and take their ball and leave the playground. Your website is just that. Your digital home base.

A blog is nice. When I say I want you to own your own home online. I mean I want you to go to dreamhost.com and buy yourself a URL. For as little as $9.99 you can own your name online and make this your digital home. TerezBaskin.com and Dbabetta.com are owned and operated by me. No one else can come and live there. No one else can take it from me. Blogger is cute, but it is owned by Google. The day Google decides to break up with Blogger there goes all your images and content with it. You ever heard of Google wave? It was all the rage in 2010, but it waved bye-bye in April of 2012. Tumblr is fun. But the day they decide that Tumblr must die, then all your reposted cute photos and content will vanish. It was recently purchased by Yahoo, so the future of tumblr is still up in the air. Remember the now defunct MySpace? I hope you understand where I am going with this. You must create a space for you, owned by you. Owned media is the most powerful space because it is yours to grow. I am sure that in 2003 when MySpace was hot, no one imagined that something else would come and take its place. You may choose to use these as platforms for your content management, but they aren't your home. You are renting space with the company. They own the building and they own your furniture.

I love Wordpress and both my Dbabetta.com blog and TerezBaskin. com are built on this easy to use content management system. I am

self-hosted, meaning I own the name and the content.
These are my digital houses and no one can take them away from me.

There is a cost to ownership, but the low expense is worth the
infinite possibilities the website will provide you. It is your 24/7
corner store. People can search for your work and understand your
POV without a conversation. They could decide to buy from you
while you are sleeping. I like that my business doesn't need my own
strength pushing it daily.

Choosing a name.

I firmly believe that owning your name is the best, most effective
way to start. I say that because your passion may change, but your
name will not. Unless you are Prince or P. Diddy, but those are
special examples. You want a name that is easy to search for and a
name that can be the best bait for Google. Yes, I know I just told you
Google wanted to steal all of your content. The truth is, they have
nailed the market on search and Google can work in your favor when
you are building a personal brand. If it isn't found on Google then
it does not really exist. Think of one of your local shops, a tire shop
or coffee house perhaps. They do great work, they may be very well
respected, yet if I can't find them online then they don't exist beyond
your neighborhood.

This naming idea is a serious one. I want you to begin with your end
in mind. How do you become the first ever Terez Baskin? You make
that name a household name by driving it home again and again. So
consistency is key. Your name on Twitter should be the same as your
name on Facebook, as on Pinterest, and Bloom. Building a brand is
about consistency in your message. You can find me by searching
Google under Terez Baskin. Here is what a recent search yielded.

You see my LinkedIn profile. There is my author link on Lucky Magazine's Community Blog. Then Twitter. Three great ways to instantly verify who I am and what I do.

I want you to be able to talk the walk. So that when people meet you out and you say, "Oh, I am an MUA. I've worked with X, Y, and Z." They know that you are about your business. They know that you are who you say that you are. Google searches are your instant digital credit rating and credibility card. I want it to make you a success and highlight your true talent. I want people to decide to work with you and spend money with you while you sleep. That is how other entrepreneurs do it. What do you think keeps you from profiting from their already proven system? Check out this resource to get you going with a shiny new website.

To find out how to get started on a blog platform and which to choose. Blogger v Wordpress: Which Is The Best Platform For Your Blog? - Epreneur TV http://ow.ly/mgJZ8

γ⁺

Tool - 11
You Are the Best Beauty Tool in Your Box!

Social media can drastically change your business for the better. If used correctly it could help you to make money while you sleep. That's what it should do. It will take some time and effort on your part, but once you have rolled that huge rock up the hill it will become easier on the way down. People will want to connect as opposed to being asked. People will see you as the expert just because you are. Your knowledge and hard work will pay off in more ways than you ever imaged. I know that this new tool is the best one you have. **It's you.** You are the resource. You are already the expert artist and lover of creativity. Now sharing it with the world is the easy part. Becoming an expert was not easy. You had to work at it. Try to get the techniques down pat. Being perfect in your offline work is just as important as being perfect online. We all know horror stories of a bad beauty treatment gone wrong. Let that be your example of what not to do.

You don't have to try everything I've laid out here, but you do need to start now. Your target audience needs you. Your customers, you know them. They are everyone and they are everywhere.
As a stylist, everyone who has or wants hair is your customer. As a nail tech, everyone with hands. For you MUAs, pretty much everyone has a face. If you don't see a person as a blank canvas for you to play with, then you are missing money and the ultimate opportunity to grow your business in a serious way.

I believe that you can do it. I am giving you permission to be great. Remember, you signed an agreement with me at the beginning of this book. After all, you did the hard part already. I bet you are thinking, how do I get started? What should I be doing? Make social media apart of your everyday business plan. Just try.

Tweets gain excitement. Facebook posts get likes and shares.

Pinterest's click-through rates are through the roof lately. Do not over -think it. Try updates that work.

Try the color of the year. Talk about trends of the moment. New styling techniques and tips. Share photos of dramatic, inspiring look and help gain exposure for your work. You slap a link right there and it will read for Twitter. Why? Because you are the expert. You are my backstage pass to the beauty industry. You know how to help make me look and feel my best.

People care about what you are doing. People want to engage and know the scoop. Give as much as you can to feed the beast. If it is not you then they will eat somewhere else.

During the day use Twitter and Instagram to continue the conversation. A photo of your set up at the shoot, I would like to see that. Maybe a quick shot of the behind-the-scenes team. Action shots are awesome for people. Are you prepping a model's face? Do you know how exciting prepping a face can look to me? Well it is all in how you spin it.

Stage your Instagram shots. Product shots are also great! There are plenty of amazing resources that can give you inspiration and tips on how to grow your Instagram audience. Think of this as your personal professional picture show. You can go now, and be amazing. I believe in you.

Your Y+ Strategy (the Formulas)

Pick a topic. Make an exhaustive list of ideas around this topic. Get specific as possible because depending on how narrow you get it will actually free your mind to explore more details within the topic.

For each blog post, brainstorm different angles for social media updates.

Facebook: Larger high quality images, include a short catchy phrase or preview sentences from the post.

Twitter: The title (make it good) + Link + #hashtag

Pinterest: Large high quality photo + good description + #hashtag. Photos will automatically link back to your blog post.

Instagram: Detail picture or collage with simple description to go to your blog post. Please note, links don't work on Instagram yet.

Beautylish: Video or Image for your profile. Link back to your blog.

Vine: Quick Video of the "Photoshoot" for the Blog post. #hashtags put you in conversations

Bloom.com: Load the picture to a LookBook. Encourage others to press the "Looks Good" button.

Google+: Share it with your circles who would be interested. Large photos + #hashtags will drive serachability. Links back to your blog will help with SEO.

The Beauty Experts' Experience

During this amazing process I had the honor and privilege of speaking to three distinct beauty industry powerhouse experts. All who are rocking the digital space and using their influence to build a brand in unique ways. All using the tools discussed in this book to craft their own unique and successful business models. I hope they inspire and excite you as much as they have for me.

Instagram: http://instagram.com/michaelduenas
Facebook: https://www.facebook.com/HairRoomService
YouTube: http://www.youtube.com/user/hairroomservice

Michael Duenas is the CEO of Hair Room Service based in New York city, but built for an international marketplace. His global scope sends him where the work is. By traveling on assignments to A-list clients like Lady Gaga to Padma Lakshmi of Top Chef, to Tiffani Thiessen of White Collar. He's done it all. His competent hand and his team have done runways and magazine galore. The best thing about him is he is not lighting his candle under a rock. He's showing his work to the world via social media.

With ten years in the game he's hitting his career stride and using social media to grow his brand. Through YouTube, Instagram, and Facebook he shares his daily journey as a jet set artist who's arrived. When I asked him how he fell into using social media for business he said that he didn't have a plan, but Michael knew that people were using social media in the fashion world and wanted to share is work. He was excited to see how receptive people were to his social media usage. "People love to know what is going on in your world", said MD. It is voyeurism at its best. I always enjoy following Michael and the Hair Room Service team. I love to see what they are working on.

When I asked what his goals were for social media markcting for HRS, he said, "I would love to continue to see our audience grow." He sees the potential, but has never considered it a marketing goal for HRS. I felt like our conversation was an eye opener. He was quiet and introspective. I think this was the first time someone asked if he was using social media platforms with the intention to make more money flow into his business. He said that he would "love to book more jobs and gain more exposure from social media."

For Micheal, the most exciting part of his digital life, is being able to share and educate younger artists. It is rewarding to know that people love your work.

I think unintentionally he and the rest of the Hair Room Services crew is on the right track. They are using the team approach to update the company's facebook page. This allows the responisblity to be even, while MD himself manages his own Instagram and the Hair Room Service Twitter account. I love the photos they take. Great clarity and focus. They are never blurry. You will see editorial shots to behind the scenes after a shoot. You can see the hairstyles clearly because the hair is the star of his show.

I know Michael has some really good projects on the horizon. I can't wait to see how social media tags along on Michael's continuing growing social story. It is an exciting time for his business and I am excited how he wows us all next.

Instagram: http://instagram.com/beautybrain24_7/
Bloom: http://www.bloom.com/bloom-story/
Twitter: https://twitter.com/BloomJulie

A serial CEO with an eye for trends, **Julie Mahloch's** Bloom.com is a revolutionary idea that underscores the power of the social media sale. Although not a superstar social media user, she understood a key component how consumers interact online.Julie caught on to the idea of social commerce, our friends and trust agents influence our purchases. She understood the connectedness of your recommendation to my purchase. For example, I wanted a pink lip color for months. I tried and tested everything from store brands to specialty stores. Nothing. Then I stumbled upon a blog post by a UK beauty blogger about this new Chanel shade of pink. I feverishly searched for it. That recommendation changed my shopping habit.

Julie predicted that this trend was going to be more powerful than any piece of advertising. The idea that your circle has more influence on where we go and what we buy. The question then became, was there a place to recommend the beauty products we loved? Was there a space where I could connect with people who could give me suggestions The question then became, was there a place to recommend the beauty products I love? Was there a space that I could connect with people who could give me suggestions on what worked for them and why? What if that recommendation came from a beauty professional? Would it hold more weight? Depending on the person, it does.

I am one of those people who enjoy reading the comments on clothes before I buy online. How did it fit? Did it run big? Small? I'm looking for keywords that work for me. Sometimes the most helpful comments are what people didn't like. I will buy a dress if you say there was too much room at the top. I am busty and I hate always going up a dress size to accommodate my top half. Social influence makes quite a larger impact than we think.

After all the research it all came together at 2 a.m. in a Vegas Nightclub.

Julie is a savvy, seasoned entrepreneur, and after all the research about a new business venture and where to go next, but it all came down to a 2 a.m. conversation in a packed Las Vegas nightclub. When two groups of women can only talk about their most recent spa treatments and beauty items they love! This flipped the switch. Julie knew that if advice from others were this strong, to keep a spirited conversation going at this hour amongst strangers. Beauty was the next industry for her and Bloom.com was born. Julie predicted Bloom was going to be the glue that connected brands, beauty professionals, and people who enjoyed their work. Their "Looks Good" button helps the bloom team understand the trends. These actions help the bloom team drive engagement around trends in the industry. I asked Julie why she thought the beauty industry was

behind the curve on social media. She believed that there were several factors. First, being that beauty professionals didn't need the Internet to be great at what they did behind the chair. It has always been an in-person business. She also believed, that more access to good and inexpensive technology like mobile devices have helped change the accessibility of their work in real-time. Lastly, she thinks that as we started to see fashion take off, the beauty industry had a harder time getting started because of the old guard at brands and major stylists. They didn't want to change.

Some people don't know how to use the tools, and therefore work around them. She sees that the biggest growth in Bloom users to be young professionals. They have a solid foundation to capture beauty programs, hair schools, and barber colleges. She is betting that if professionals are caught early on, they can grow their skills online and offline together as they grow into a professional career. Bloom also allows these new professionals to keep in touch beauty lovers. It is about forming a habit and building loyalty on the new platform. She wants to see it continue to grow into a positive business need from pros and brands alike. As they continue to change and grow they are able to offer more digital services to professionals who want to challenge their current business model. Bloom is on trend to continue to transform the industry.

Twitter: https://twitter.com/GlobalGirl_LA
Pinterest: http://pinterest.com/globalgirlla/
Website: https://www.facebook.com/pages/Social-Global-Grind/148473468554006

The last expert I want to share with you is a global social butterfly. I think she is my business soul sister. She is an entrepreneur who transitioned into business after a successful career as a master makeup artist for Mac cosmetics. I found our conversation refreshing like a cucumber mask on a hot day! All I could do was agree, feverishly shaking my head, and smile. Laugh and yell YESSS YUP! That's it! Francesca Alexander is the CEO of Global Social Grind, a social media public relations firm specializing in the beauty industry. Many of her clients are beauty professionals like you. They go to her lost, and gain a better understanding of how to manage and market their business in a digital world.

Francesca understands the behind-the-chair life. She was a makeup artist who understood the business behind being a brand. Being an artist was only part of the story. Francesca believed and still preaches that you have to be able to run your business in a way that makes the most sense for you. She says that beauty experts are afraid to be the experts. They believe that their training makes them better than a blogger, but the difference between them and that blogger is that the blogger is courageous. They are fearless in the digital space and are ready and willing to make mistakes. "Being a risk-taker is what puts money in your pocket. Playing it safe will never take you where you want to go", said Francesca.

She explained that the birth of social media and digital business, everything moves at the speed of light. I asked her what advice she gives to beauty professionals who say they don't need the web to do their work. She cautions her clients about being behind the times. She said bluntly: "Do you think you can go out and get an ad in the newspaper? Will people be able to look you up in the phone book? Do not kid yourself into thinking you can continue to wait for permission to get started."

She urges professionals that if they want to be taken seriously by the brands, business, fashion designers, and television executives then they need to start speaking the language of business, and it is digital. No one will wait a week for you to send your portfolio in the mail. You will be passed over again and again. "Use Facebook, blog, take pictures with Instagram," she says. She knows how busy beauty professionals are. She recommends scheduling time on Sunday to write, schedule blog posts, and upload photos. Once you get into the groove then it will be easier and easier to stay on top of it. Soon she will be launching her Hustle and Glow mentorship program where you can get her concentrated goodness live and direct injected into your business. I highly recommend you see what is up next for this high-powered girl on the go.

What is next for you?

Now that you know what to do and how to do it. Just get started

A YEAR FROM NOW
YOU WILL WISH
YOU HAD STARTED TODAY.
- KAREN LAMB

XO,
Terez

www.ingramcontent.com/pod-product-compliance
Lightning Source LLC
Chambersburg PA
CBHW041716200326
41519CB00005B/269